CONFUSED

PRINCIPLES FOR LIVING CHRISTIAN IN A
CHAOTIC WORLD

ANDREA GADSON

CONFUSED?

Principles for Living Christian in a Chaotic World

ANDREA GADSON

SurrenderedPen Publishing

Confused

Copyright © 2019 by Andrea Gadson

This edition: ISBN 978-0-9898301-5-7 (soft cover)

Printed in the United States of America

www.surrenderedpen.com

Dedication

For my sister Sandra.

May I live my life in a way that honors you always.

CONTENTS

FOREWORD

Dear Reader,

I don't want to make an assumption that you are a Christian. While you may have picked up this book for a number of reasons, it's important to me to make sure you know how to receive Christ. We simplify how to receive Christ by referring to the A-B-C method:

- **Accept** that you are separated from God and living in disobedience to him, which is called sin
- **Believe** Jesus died for you, and through his death, resurrection and ascension to heaven you have the opportunity for restored relationship with God
- **Confess** your belief with your mouth; heart-fully accept Jesus as the one you will model your life after

The last one can be accomplished through a simple prayer which you can say right now. Repeat this aloud:

Jesus I need you. I know from birth I have lived a life separated from you. But I believe you gave up your life for this moment in my life. Because you died for me, came back to life, and now sit in heaven with God, I don't have to live like this. I invite you into my life. I invite you to take control of my life. Thank you and Amen.

It's that simple. A-B-C. Your next steps include:

1. *Find a good church home.* This should be a place where they teach the Bible, which is your guidebook on how to live as a believer in Christ.
2. *Read the Bible daily.* Don't just take my word or the word of others. Anytime you hear something, read it for yourself. In reading on your own, start with the New Testament in the section titled "John" and keep going on from there.
3. *Start talking with God daily.* This is all about praying, which is talking to God about what you read in his Bible. Talk to him about what's in your heart. Talk to him about your needs. Talk to him about everything and anything. He's ready to listen and to help.
4. *Put godly people around you.* To help you grow as a Christian, add godly people to the list of influencers in your life and spend time learning from them.

God Bless,
Andrea

1 INTRODUCTION

God is not complicated.

It took me a long time to realize this.

As a young woman, I wanted a close relationship with God, but I was not sure how to get there. My solution — read every book I could find to help me grow as a Christian.

By the end of some of those books, I believed I had to do everything I read to be close to God. I was afraid to mess up. When I did, I was a ridiculous lump of emotions. Eventually, I became judgmental of myself and others. You can imagine what happens when your mind gets away from you.

What was I thinking?

God is not complicated, but in my quest to be a better person, to draw closer to him, I complicated him. I complicated being a Christian.

Overwhelmed, I knew I could never measure up. I would never be "good enough." Unsurprisingly, I decreased my Bible reading and praying. My logic — the less I knew, the better the opportunity to get it right.

I wouldn't say I walked away from God. Instead, I tried to hide. The weird part is I hid in all my "Christian" activities. Forget about having a close relationship. At least I was doing a bunch of tasks for him. Wasn't this the same as being close?

Light switch moments

Fortunately, one day, something clicked inside of me. Nothing spectacular. Like a light switch illuminating a dark room, in a moment, I became clearly aware of the fact that God is not complicated. I like to think it was God showing mercy and saving me from myself.

I am thankful for the light switch moment. Without it, I would be floundering in confusion. Instead of getting closer, I would be standing at a distance gripping my fear of failing him.

Many Christians, new and seasoned, need light switch moments to define and clarify their relationship with God. A new Christian may need such a moment to assure a right start in their relationship with God. A seasoned Christian may need such a moment to restore or refresh a relationship with him.

A love letter

What if God wrote a brief letter to you to turn on a light switch? I've been thinking about what this love letter would contain.

It might sound like this:

Dear One I Love,

I am not complicated. You don't need an advanced degree to experience me. No need to worry about doing it just right to win my love. You already have my love. The relationship we need to have is very simple. It is one where I love you. I want your love. And I want you to love others.

Next, I think he would sign it something like,

To My Love,
Your God

Amazing. If I read such a letter in my youth, I would have avoided many days of worry and disappointment.

What would God mean by the last three sentences? Can a relationship with Him be that simple? He loves us. He wants our love. He wants us to love others.

It can't be that simple.

Or can it?

2 STARTING WITH THE FOUNDATIONS

I know I am not the only person who ever complicated God. Be honest. Have you done it to some degree?

We live in a society where being complicated seems to have more value. The more difficult something seems, the more importance we give it.

We add so much to God's requirements that it looks a little like spaghetti. We have no idea where it ends or begins. My heart tells me this was not God's plan when he created us.

The Basics

Basic ('bāsik) - the essential facts or principles of a subject or skill

---

Life is better when we stick to the basics. Generally, we define basics as the simple foundations, the simple ways of doing things. Everything else flows from these foundations.

We can achieve a more abundant life if we focus on God's basics and let everything we do and say flow from them.

We need to get back to the basics regarding relationship with God. **When he created us, his intention was to have a relationship.** From the beginning, this is what he wanted.

We can achieve relationship through the three simple truths in the love letter I proposed earlier.

God loves us.
God wants our love.
God wants us to love others.

Everything in the Bible links to these three points. These truths are the basics — the foundation or building blocks for how we create and keep a relationship with God.

Consider This

Our inner selves are constantly longing for something. No amount of what we try with today's solutions fits or totally fulfills that longing. People marry and divorce and fall in and out of social entertainment, technology and media fads because they are trying to satisfy their inner desire. People keep writing and reading the same self-help books in pursuit of inner satisfaction. We keep recreating the same motivational message in different packages trying to find the final formula to complete our inner selves.

Ecclesiastes 3:11 NKJV tells us God placed eternity in our hearts. I believe he put some of his eternal power in us, which generates a longing to connect back to him. This act of giving us a bit of himself reminds me of the half-a-heart necklace. One person wears one half, while someone else, usually someone they deeply love, wears the other half. We are always looking for the other half of our heart. Guess what? God Almighty is wearing the other half.

Our inner self is seeking the other half of our hearts and we won't be satisfied until we get it.

Getting back to the basics with these three truths is about matching to the other half of our heart. It's about going back to our first and true love, which is The Lord, God, who created us.

3   GOD IS LOVE

Before I married, my definition of love was the version from the movies. You know it. Boy meets girl. After the initial clumsiness and mixed messages, they learn more about each other. From there, they plunge into a set of emotions which they call love. During this journey, they must express their love through a sexual encounter. Without this they cannot possibly love each other, right? By the end of the movie, the couple rides off into a happily ever after sunset.

As you can see, my mind was in another world, and it was not the real world. By pursuing love in this fashion, I always landed in one of several scenarios:

- I loved someone who didn't love me back
- I defined love by how much the person did for me
- I only loved when loved in return
- I believed sex = love
- I thought if no one loves me, I was not worthy of love

What a perfect list of ingredients for a recipe called ***confusion***.

Before we go further, it may be helpful to review a key principle — **God is love**. Another way to write it is:

$$God = Love$$

First John 4:16 NKJV states, "And we have known and believed the love that God has for us. God is love, and he who abides in love abides in God, and God in him."

God is all about love. It can't get any simpler than that, but what is love?

What is love?

God gives a clear definition of love in 1 Corinthians 13 NIV. He says love is patient. Love is kind. It does not envy. It does not boast. It is not proud. It is not rude. It is not selfish. It doesn't get angry easily. It does not keep a record of the wrongs. Love does not delight in evil but rejoices in the truth. It always protects, always trusts, always hopes, and always perseveres. Love never fails.

These characteristics demonstrate the intense and powerful nature of love. They show the limitless boundaries of love. And if God is love, then he's got to be all these characteristics.

I'll prove my point by getting a little geeky for a moment.

A little geeky

If you remember some of your high school math, you may recall an algebra equation which went something like this:

$$\text{If } a=b \text{ and } b=c \text{ then } a=c$$

Therefore, when we do the math, if God is love, and love is all these things. Then God is all these things. God is patient. God is kind. God does not envy. God does not boast. God is not proud. God is not rude. God is not selfish. God is not easily angered. God does not keep a record of wrongs. God does not delight in evil but rejoices in truth. He always protects, always trusts, always hopes. God always perseveres. God never fails.

God is love, and his actions toward us are *love-based* and *love-soaked*. In love, I believe God formed the first man and woman. In love, God guided and protected the Old Testament Jewish community across a desert. In love, God sent prophets and teachers. In love, God appointed Christ to a task for all peoples. In love, God will renew the earth. All in love and because of love.

Really? Love without conditions?

I often think God's love is a little beyond our comprehension. We define love based on our human experiences. We love our parents. We love our friends. We love our spouses. But sometimes this love comes with conditions. If they love us, we will love them. If they treat us well, we will love them. If they do not hurt us, we will love them.

But God's love is **condition-less**. We hurt him, treat him unfairly, and occasionally withdraw our love from him. Yet, he continues to pursue us, waiting for our return like the prodigal son's father (Luke 15:11-32).

If God had conditions to his love, the Bible verses in Romans 5:8 NKJV would read, "But God demonstrates his own love for us in this: While we were still in sin, Christ did <u>not</u> die for us." This would mean Christ was waiting for us to get out of sin before he helped. Instead, this verse reads as, "…in that while we were still sinners, Christ died for us." **God did not need a condition of perfection to give his love**.

We all want somebody to love us

We all want someone to love us, even the hardcore among us, who think we don't need anyone. We seek love from family and friends. We define love by their actions. We say, I know they love me because they:

- Support and commit to me
- Provide for me
- Give me things
- Said so

Funny! God does all this for us, yet we forget that he loves us. At times, family and friends remove, pull back, and throw away their love. But God will always love us. I believe his love for us is why we haven't seen the long prophesied "end of the world" yet. I believe it's coming, but God is a chance-giver. He is "patient with you, not wanting anyone to perish, but everyone to come to repentance" (2 Peter 3:9 NIV).

He gives us chances, or opportunities, to experience a loving relationship with him. It is a relationship where we don't have to worry that he will one day stop loving his creation. Note, I did not say he won't get irritated by our ways and need to correct us. Yet even his correction is a form of love.

Yes, we all want somebody to love us, and God stands in the ready position, waiting to express the characteristics of love to us. His very nature and essence are love.

Believe it or not, the basic and foundational truth is that God loves us.

4 GOD LOVES US

God loves us? More specifically, God loves me?

My life includes a period when I did not believe this. No one could make me believe it. It was impossible given my past experiences.

You see, I had been molested as a child. It transformed me into a frightened mouse, afraid to be seen or acknowledged. I constantly felt like I wanted to disappear. Solace came in the form of books and the quiet alone of my bedroom, where no one could touch me.

If you had told me then that God loved me, I would have laughed and stuck my head in a book. I did not believe anyone loved me. As I grew from teen into woman, a new mindset took over. I thought if no one cared about me, I would not care about me. My best response was to be sexually active.

When I found myself under a tree, with my bare butt pressing against the tree root and some guy, whose name I would never remember, touching me, I knew I had fully given into the idea that no one loved me. My mind told me I was a bad person; bad people were not worthy of love and God did not love bad people.

That is what I thought.

How do we know God loves us?

Let's begin with understanding God's love for us. How do we know that he loves us? Where is the proof? Well . . .

- He said so
- He created us
- He sent Jesus as a demonstration of that love
- He loved us first (way before we had a chance to return this love)
- He sees us despite ourselves

Sometimes I imagine God says I love you so much it hurts. It hurts him that we don't realize the depth, the width, and the height of that love.

Going geeky again (so sorry but I can't help it)

In school, I remember being taught the mathematical term "infinity." It is a distance that can never be reached. Imagine going on forever and never reaching the end of something. There are some things in life I would never want to have an infinite nature to them. The love of God is not one of them.

Imagine a love that has no end. Or to put it another way, a love whose end cannot be reached. A love that never runs out. A love that doesn't stop. A love that keeps loving. That's God's love for us. This doesn't mean you can do any old thing and treat God any old way. It means while you're doing your dirt, he loves you. And if he must correct your behavior or your thoughts, he still loves you.

Hey, show me the proof

First, God loves me because **he said so . . .**

The Bible is bursting with references which show God's love for us, but for me, the one which has the largest pop is John 3:16. We often repeat this scripture without hearing and seeing the words. The first part of the verse states, "God so loved the world . . ." This verse reveals God's enormous compassion for us; he has a great desire for this world and its inhabitants.

And do not forget **he created us** (Genesis 1:26-27 NKJV).

He breathed His own breath into us. His breath started our living as humanity. The process, the energy, and the time which goes into making something, often creates a natural closeness, fondness, and oneness with the creation.

Just like parents love the child they create, God loves us. The Creator said in Genesis that he wanted to make man in his image. And after he molded his creation, he loved what he made.

Next God **demonstrated his love** for us. We pick up the rest of John 3:16, and we read, ". . .he gave his only son." Any parent, who deeply cares for their child, will not sacrifice them for someone else. Many would sacrifice themselves first.

First John 4:9-10 repeats the message. God sent his only son to demonstrate how much he cares and loves us. Since the Garden of Eden catastrophe, God has been thinking about us. We are always on his mind and his heart. Jesus is his plan in response to what happened in the Garden of Eden (Genesis 1-3 NLT).

First John 4:19 tells us again that he loved us, but it adds an order effect. It says **he loved us first**. Without an initial offering of love, God extended his love toward us first. Imagine that! Before we had a chance to say, "I love you," he already loved us.

Romans 5:8 tells us God sent his only son, Jesus, to die for us while we were still doing things our way and not his way. While we were spitting in his face, he was working on a plan to show us how much he loved us. Despite what we show him day after day, **his eyes see us**. He does not see what we were; he sees what he created us to be.

All these verses, and there are hundreds more, connect to God loving us.

Pause Moment: I'm taking a moment to check in with you. I want you to read this book without any of your past hurt getting in the way. If your parents did not love you the way a parent is supposed to love their child, ask God to help. Ask him to help you let go of the fact someone did not love you. Ask him to help you let go so you can let him in. Psalm 27:10 reminds us that even if our parents abandon us [mentally, physically, emotionally, etc.], the Lord will hold us close to him.

If God loves us, then why…?

I can't close the door on this chapter without addressing something that may be on your mind.

> **If God loves me why do bad things happen to me?**
> or
> **If God loves me, why don't I have things**
> **I want or need?**

Very good questions to which I do not have the perfect answer. What I can say is that God loves us through the bad experiences and through the seasons of lack. The absence of material objects or the presence of a tough situation in our lives does not mean God does not love us.

The Bible tells us some cold hard facts and one of them is in John 16:33 NLT:

> "I have told you all this so that you may have peace in
>   me. Here on earth you will have many trials and
>   sorrows. But take heart, because I have overcome
>   the world."

The fact is being a believer in Christ and living a life modeled after Christ doesn't guarantee a trouble-free life. It does guarantee a life, where someone, i.e., the Lord Jesus, is there as a "ride or die" sidekick. He sticks with us through the uncomfortable. If we let him, he will be the driver in the getaway car which takes us out of the storms.

The experiences which happen to us are opportunities to share the light of Jesus. During these periods the promise of 2

Corinthians 4:8-10 NLT must be like a flag waving above our heads as we march through:

> "We are pressed on every side by troubles, but we are not crushed. We are perplexed, but not driven to despair. We are hunted down, but never abandoned by God. We get knocked down, but we are not destroyed. Through suffering, our bodies continue to share in the death of Jesus so that the life of Jesus may also be seen in our bodies."

These experiences are designed to make us walk away from him, but he won't walk away from us. Yes, these experiences hurt, but our pain is only for a moment compared to the joy we have. Second Corinthians 4:17 NLT says it best:

> "For our present troubles are small and won't last very long. Yet they produce for us a glory that vastly outweighs them and will last forever!"

At this point, members of the "logical mind" club (of which I am one), may be asking about why have a relationship with Christ. They may say "If I ain't gonna (grammar intended) have a trouble-free life, then why have the relationship." The answer is summarized by the word "temporary". The life we have is temporary, and the best way to live it is with Christ. The partnership we have during the temporary journey is a preparation for the partnership in the eternal journey, which has no troubles attached.

Trouble like children dying before parents. Trouble like someone causing bodily harm to you or your family. Trouble like losing jobs and security. According to 2 Corinthians 4:17, all these examples are temporary compared to eternal life with Christ.

How can she be so sure?

I am not sharing this perspective from a safe zone where nothing happens to me or to my family. The toughest questions I've had to ask is if God loves me, why didn't he protect me from childhood sexual abuse. A Mighty God could have stopped it. So why didn't he? Over the years, and still today, I am learning to embrace the following facts.

Fact #1: Love made God weep in the pain of my experience with me.

Fact #2: Love made God send Jesus for me.

Fact #3: Love wiped my mind of the horror of the experience.

Fact #4 (and this is a big one): Sin (evidence of the world I live in) sent the evil.

To understand what happened, I had to understand who controls our world today, what sin and evil does, and God's promise in times of trouble as shown in Psalm 46:1-3 NLT:

> "God is our refuge and strength, always ready to help in times of trouble. So we will not fear when earthquakes come and the mountains crumble into the sea. Let the oceans roar and foam. Let the mountains tremble as the waters surge!"

I hope this imperfect, yet faith-soaked answer, helps you receive the truth that God loves you.

The question is will you love God the way he loves you?

―――――――――

A Connection for You

Does God love you? How do you know?

Regardless if you know the answer for yourself personally or if you have doubts, spend the next 7 days engaging with the proof scriptures given to you in the chapter. Your pattern for each day will be:

1. Pray asking God to open your eyes, unstop your ears, and melt your heart so that you can see, hear and know what he wants you to see, hear and know.
2. Read the scriptures in this chapter. This is not about memorization. Read them thoroughly as if it is the first time you're seeing them each time.
3. Pray again and thank God for making these verses a part of your day.

A Starter Prayer
(I'll start, and you take over)

If you struggle with believing or accepting God's love for you, I offer this prayer as help:

Lord of all things. I know you love me. But still doubt is trying to overcome me. The things I've been through are telling me you don't love me. Show me, Holy Spirit, how to overcome these thoughts and feelings. Help me to overcome these thoughts and feelings. I know how David felt in Psalm 13 when he went through the same doubt but now I say to you the final verses. I will also trust in your unfailing love. I will sing your praise because you have been good to me. Help me, Dear Helper, to live and breathe what I am saying. I pray by the Powerful and Loving Name of Jesus.

If you are certain of God's love for you, I offer this celebratory prayer for you:

Lover of my soul. This name perfectly describes what I know. You are the beginning and end of my life. You are my friend. You are my guide. No one can love me the way you do. I am so happy knowing that if you are for me, it does not matter who is against me, I have confidence in knowing no trouble or hardship or persecution or lack or danger or death can separate me from your love. I pray by the Powerful and Loving Name of Jesus.

5   GOD WANTS OUR LOVE

When I was younger, I worked with the street evangelism team in my church. We would knock on doors of people's home and share who Christ was with them. Sometimes I met people who said they weren't ready for Christ. They believed he was the Son of God, but they did not feel ready for him. Often, these people were referring to needing the right clothing or hairstyle or lifestyle in order to enter a church building. They believed until they got these items, they had nothing to offer God.

Many people have a perspective that God is mighty and powerful, and, in comparison, humans are puny and weak.

With this perspective, we wonder why would God want anything from us? Can we possibly give him something he needs?

The following verses tell us what God wants from us.

Deuteronomy 6:5 NKJV

> "You shall love the Lord your God with all your heart, with all your soul, and with all your strength."

Matthew 22:37 NKJV

> 'Jesus said to him, "You shall love the Lord your God with all your heart, with all your soul, and with all your mind."'

Mark 12:29-30 NKJV

> "Jesus answered him, "The first of all the commandments is: 'Hear, O Israel, the Lord our God, the Lord is one. And you shall love the Lord your God with all your heart, with all your soul, with all your mind, and with all your strength.' This is the first commandment."

Luke 10:27 NIV

> 'So he answered and said, "You shall love the Lord your God with all your heart, with all your soul, with all your strength, and with all your mind,' and 'your neighbor as yourself."'

God says love me with all you got. Pour all of you into all of me. At no time when God gave us his truths did he say they would be easy to follow. In fact, they are hard to follow. It takes time. It takes discipline and commitment. Some truths come easily, but we may spend a lifetime aiming at others and missing. God never said it would be easy. There you have it; I've said it. You finally heard me say it. Let's put that to the side for a moment.

I believe God knew it would be hard to follow the basics. He knew it would be impossible if we do not see him as worthy of our love. We covered what makes him worthy when we looked at how he loves us in the prior chapter. Isn't someone who sacrificed his son for you, loves you as you are, and sees all of you and still cares about you, worthy of even a fraction of your love?

The key to success is to pour ourselves into him and love him unto "death", that is unto our own physical end and to the end of our own internal desires.

When we love with human love, we pour ourselves into people, animals, and even inanimate objects. When we love with great intensity, giving all of ourselves to something, we think about our love object all the time. We act with our love object in mind. When love is this powerful, we forget about ourselves and solely seek what elevates, protects, encourages, and promotes the object of our love.

Love me with all you got

God tells me to love him with all I got. What do I have?

- My **heart**, which is the **seat of my emotions**, and I

must give it to him <u>freely</u> and <u>fully</u>. My heart is where my pain and my joy live. It is the place of my desires, feelings, affections, passions, and impulses. My heart is where my love begins and grows. When I love the Lord with all my heart, I wrap myself around him, and my emotions are not about me. They are about him. I long for him. I crave him. I desire his respect. I wish only to please him. These actions come from giving all my heart to God.

- My **soul**, which is the **seat of my actions**, and I must give it to him <u>freely</u> and <u>fully</u>. My soul is where I decide right from wrong. My heart and my soul are connected. As my emotions release, they run to the soul for justification, vindication, and for decision. My soul is the place where my ideas are born. It is the place where some ideas die. When I give all my soul to the Lord, it is an example of sweet and total surrender. I put my actions in the palm of his hands. That's loving with all my soul.

- My **mind**, which is the **seat of my thinking**, and I must give it to him <u>freely</u> and <u>fully</u>. My mind is where I take the ideas which did not die in my soul and give them life. I turn them over in my mind. I plan their course. Sometimes I make elaborate plans; other times I do quick hits. My mind and my soul are connected. Once I work through ideas, I give them back to the soul to put into action. When I love God with all my mind, I drench my thinking with Him. When I make plans, I do so with a full awareness of him. He is the reminder in my thinking; he is the security guard of my thinking.

- My **strength**, which is the **seat of my will**, and I must give it to him freely and fully. My strength is the degree to which I will love the Lord. With my strength, I dictate the intensity of my action. In giving all my strength, I exercise an unbreakable and unshakeable will to love him.

God wants all my love in the form of *all of me*. He never said give me your heart, and you can have the rest. This is the definition of division. It would never be successful. God wants us to do the basics, the foundational truths. He knows we cannot do this if we are partially participating.

Demonstrating love to God

When I consider how to show my love to God, three "throughs" come to mind:

- *Through* obedience
- *Through* praise and worship
- *Through* thanks

Through obedience – God says if you love me, you will keep my principles. The word He uses is commandments, but I think some of you might complain about being commanded to do something. God's commandments are simply guidance for how to live your life.

Through praise and worship – Honestly, everyone likes to be adored and recognized for their accomplishments. Since God created us in his image, he too desires adoration and recognition. We have evidence of his accomplishments in the Bible. But personally, he has done far more than you will ever know.

He prevented certain events from happening to you; others he helped you bear, although you may think you did it all on your own. He is worthy of praise and worship.

Through thanks – Thanking someone is an acknowledgment of appreciation for what they've done for you. While praise and worship recognize power and skill, thankfulness takes the relationship to another level. Thanksgiving moves the heart into a position of total surrender. True, deep down thanks to God indicates you know that no one but him did something for you.

God does not need our love, but he sure does want it.

Love is about relationship. Relationship has two sides – God and me. God keeps his part when he shows us he loves us. We keep our part when we fulfill the desire of love God wants from us. Remember – God does not need our love, but he sure does want it.

A Connection for You

Is there an area where you are not showing love to God? Are you lacking in praise and worship? Are you lacking in being thankful? Has your obedience been a little on the weak side? Now is a good time to:

1. Acknowledge the area where you haven't been showing love towards God.

2. Check out your heart. Do you want to love God in this way? Often this means giving up something you want and replacing it with something better — what God wants.

3. After you've done the first two, ask God for the ability to love him in the area of lack. If you're having a hard time forgiving the way he wants you to, ask him for help to do it. This kind of prayer is one God does not turn down. Therefore, the 4th step is crucial.

4. Accept God's answer to your prayer. Embrace what he gives you for overcoming the area you lack.

A Starter Prayer
(I'll start, and you take over)

My Creator. My Friend. It amazes me to know someone as awesome and as powerful as you would want love from me. I will do my best to give you my love through my obedience, my praise and worship and my thankfulness. And when I fail, I will use my failure to draw closer to you. Through your Holy Spirit please show me daily how to love you.
In Jesus' precious Name I pray.

6   GOD WANTS US TO LOVE OTHERS

The last principle is probably the most difficult of the three basics. Loving others is hard enough when they are family, but it is more challenging when they are strangers, and seemingly impossible when they are unlikeable.

My first experience with loving someone unlikeable came in a work environment. It was my first job in a professional setting. I was young and eager to please. My manager told me the first part of my assignment was to become familiar with a new system. When I reported I had learned enough and was ready to start using the system, he shared the second part of the assignment. I remember the atmosphere shifting into a somber and fearful quiet as everyone in our small office listened in on our conversation, and my manager told me the second part of my assignment was Brenda Johnson (not her real name).

I had not met Brenda yet. I did not know who she was, but warning bells rang in my ears and my heart swelled as blood raced through it at an alarming rate. My manager informed me about Brenda's background. He shared why most people feared her and did not want to work with her.

Brenda was a woman in her late 40s with a strong opinion on everything and a mouth which was not afraid to share that opinion. Brenda was every information technology department's nightmare customer. She hated change. She hated technology. She hated people who represented change and technology both. And…she had POWER.

The next part of my assignment was to teach the new system from my department, which was information technology, to Brenda Johnson.

As we navigate what it means to love others, and before I tell you what happened with Brenda, remember the definition of love we reviewed earlier from 1 Corinthians 13:4-8 NIV:

> "Love is patient. Love is kind. It does not envy. It does
> not boast. It is not proud. It is not rude. It is not
> selfish. It doesn't get angry easily. It does not keep
> a record of the wrongs. Love does not delight in
> evil but rejoices in the truth. It always protects,
> always trusts, always hopes, and always perseveres.
> Love never fails."

God is all about relationships

We are social people. God made us this way. In the Garden of Eden, Adam needed companionship. God made Eve. Although we use the creation of Eve as the example of marriage, it's also an example of the importance of relationship. We need connection with other people. God wired us this way.

But why? Because relationships are the key part of how we love him. We demonstrate our love for him in how we love others. We spread our affection for him to others. If we do it right, i.e., the First Corinthians 13 way, we change ourselves and the world around us.

How do we know God wants us to love others?

The proof is once again in the Bible. Jesus tells us who to love and how to love them.

Love your neighbor as yourself.
(Leviticus 19:18; Matthew 22:39; Mark 12:31)

"Your neighbor" is the "who."

"As you love yourself" is the "how."

Who is our neighbor?

In Luke 10:29-37 NIV, Jesus tells a story which clearly defines who our neighbor is. You should read the story because the summary I provide in this book is weak, admittedly. In the story, a stranger gives his money and time to help another stranger when that man gets robbed. These two men did not know each other, but the one showed mercy and kindness to the other. Mercy and kindness are elements of love. Jesus uses the story to establish that everyone, from your mother to the person who sits next to you on the bus trip to work, is your neighbor.

Love yourself first

For a moment. I want to focus on the second part of the verses in Luke 10:27 NKJV:

> So he answered and said, "'You shall love the Lord your God with all your heart, with all your soul, with all your strength, and with all your mind,' and 'your neighbor as yourself.' "

This reference to love your neighbor like you love yourself can also be found in Matthew 19:19, Galatians 5:14, and James 2:8.

We must love people in the same way we love ourselves. You may not want to sound selfish, but the truth is when you love yourself you take good care of you. You respect yourself. You care about what happens to you. You make yourself a priority. This is how you need to take care of others.

If you just said aloud or in your head "But what if I don't like myself?", then you may have a problem bigger than the pages of this book. I said it was big but not insurmountable.

The inability to love yourself is a problem which plagues many people. It may have begun during childhood or developed later in life. Experiences or relationships may be a huge part of the challenge. I remember my own period of inability to love myself. I thought I was unlovable because of my past childhood experiences. I thought I wasn't enough. Not pretty enough. Not friendly enough. Not talented enough. One truth which pulled me past the "not enough" period into a period of acceptance was something I had to remind myself of repeatedly.

Not liking myself was like disliking what God created.

God created me. Life tried to disfigure me. I had to allow God to heal me.

Take time to get to the source of your dislike. Too many times we treat the symptoms of our ailments but never look at the source. Ask:

- Why do I dislike myself?
- Is there something in my life or behavior which needs to be addressed?
- How can I start liking me?

The key to loving others is to know how to love yourself. You may need to chat with someone like a spiritual mentor or a professional to help you through this process.

But what's next? Should you wait until you know how to love yourself before you love others? Or, should you start loving others and wait for a breakthrough of loving yourself to happen is the midst of this?

I'm going to say the words I hate to hear, but they apply to each situation they are uttered in — it depends. It depends on you.

To illustrate this, I will share my personal experience. I am a rule-oriented person. Tell me the rule, and I'll do my best to follow it. What worked for me was to find out how to love people and then get cracking at it. Although I had days when I couldn't stand myself, it was easier to work for the betterment of others. It was easier to focus on others. However, this wasn't sustainable for the long haul. When I didn't get the love I gave out in return, I blamed myself. In order to love others better, I had to learn to love myself. Ironic, isn't it? Loving others showed me how to love myself.

This worked for me. Please identify what works for you. If you determine you need to work on loving yourself first, start working on it and try loving others a little bit at a time while you're doing it.

How do we love everyone?

Loving people is about practicing some portion of 1 Corinthians 13. (Read it for yourself now.) As we increase our practice, we deepen our relationship with others. It is a gradual process.

Please don't shut down right now. Please remove all your excuses. Remember if you love God and hate others, then you don't love God. It's impossible according to 1 John 4:20 NIV:

"Whoever claims to love God yet hates a brother or
sister is a liar. For whoever does not love their
brother and sister, whom they have seen, cannot
love God, whom they have not seen."

Using the word liar may sound harsh, but this is serious business. *God needs you to love others as a way of loving him and promoting who he is to others.* If you have a problem connecting to yourself, get working fast so you can do what God wants you to do.

Yeah, yeah, I got it. But…

But what about those unlikeable folks like Brenda Johnson.

I'm pretty sure by now some of you are asking how to love someone when you don't like them, and even more, when they are a real enemy?

I don't want to sound flippant, trite, naive, or any word that may sound like I don't get it. Believe me I do. I've had some people in my life who were unlikeable. One person I recall was somewhat antagonistic, but his aggression came with a smile on his face as he looked for ways to challenge my Christianity. Whenever he felt an urge come over him, he would approach me with a question or statement about my beliefs. Sometimes he presented awful jokes with a biblical reference. Sometimes it was a comment about what science had found about some biblical fact like the parting of the Red Sea or Noah's ark.

I wanted to go head on with this gentleman. I wanted to demean him and tell him about all the pain and darkness in his life which caused him to be negative at times. I wanted to hurt him like he successfully hurt me occasionally.

My biggest option was to pray for him.

This is how we are to love on people we don't like or who are our enemies. We pray for them. Offer kindness, even when you get no kindness in return (Matthew 5:43-45 NKJV). Do your best not to get easily angered by them, and so on. You remember the formula. Trust God to protect you when your enemy is out to destroy you.

Loving someone as 1 Corinthians 13 describes is difficult to do in a cold, harsh world. Some people seem to find it easier to hate than to show love; hating comes easier and requires far less work. But it's never as fulfilling as loving someone.

God built us to be social, loving folks.

Am I crazy?

No, I'm not. I'm a realist. I do not always get this right. Between you, these pages, and me, there are days when I want to run my car into the bumper of someone who nearly pushed my car out of a lane with their car. There are times when I want to slap someone's cell phone out of their hand as they stand near me on an elevator yapping into the mouthpiece. And, there are moments when I am just as rude to someone as they are to me. Working the basics requires practice. The more I practice loving people, the more I'm able to overcome these moments.

Back to Brenda

Returning to my story about Brenda Johnson, I trudged, and I do mean trudged, down to Brenda's cube. My feet felt like I was wearing cement coated shoes. I hated confrontation, and I wondered what kind of people would send a young, naive girl into a battle many of them had either lost or returned from with permanent bruising.

Brenda Johnson had a short stature and a powerful tongue. The gritty look in her eyes displayed her distaste for my chore long before she opened her mouth to tell me she did not like my department or our systems.

I had not yet read 1 Corinthians 13, but I do believe God had been leading me to Jesus for a long time before I decided to live my life in Jesus. In those first moments with Brenda Johnson, I began to "kill her with kindness". I was patient. I did not get angry. I was not rude. I let go the record of wrong when Brenda snapped at me. I told Brenda I understood her challenges. I praised her when she did something right in the system. By the end of the afternoon, Brenda was telling me she needed to remove her shoes because her feet were sore from wearing them all day. We had become such good friends and, in the end, Brenda was comfortable with me.

I learned to love this way because of Brenda.

Here's the final word

Every moment with the Brendas of our lives will not have such a great ending, but the final say-so on this principle of God wanting us to love others is 1 John 4:21 NKJV:

> "And this commandment we have from Him: that he who loves God must love his brother also."

To know God is to love like God. And God loves people.

A Connection for You

Practice is the key. Practice in small ways to build to the big ways.

Practice giving love before it's returned to you. The following *small recommendations* build a habit which makes it easier to gradually move into loving regularly in the *big ways*.

Here are just a few ways to show love:

- Allow someone to merge in front of you in traffic.
- Purchase a cup of coffee or tea for a stranger in front of you in line.
- Say "hello" and "thank you" more often.
- Send a card to someone before there's a reason to send one; the card could be a "thinking about you" or "just praying for you" card.
- Sweep the sidewalk in front of your neighbor's pavement (in winter this would be shoveling the snow from their sidewalk).
- When someone is rude to you, return the rudeness with a completely opposite reaction, i.e., not rudeness.
- Replace an opportunity to gossip about someone with the opportunity to pray for them.
- When driven to say a negative word, replace it with a positive word.

It's about spotting opportunities to *show love before there is a need for* it. And *giving love when there is a need for it.*

Finally, if you are having trouble liking yourself, seek help from a spiritual mentor or a professional. Don't take another step alone.

A Starter Prayer
(I'll start, and you take over)

Dear Orchestrator of my Life, I confess that on some days and in some seasons of my life, I do not feel very loving. I recognize these are the moments where I will need your strength to love the way you want me to love. I like being selective in giving my love because I can choose the easiest targets to give my love to. Right now, I surrender to you my strong desire to be in control of when, who and how to love. Loving someone who loves me is easy. I need your help to be the kind of person who loves all the time. I want to love in order to show you to others. I need help to live the way I want to love. Please help me. In the Name of Jesus.

7 THAT'S IT

That's it!

Three simple basics. I agree there will be times when it will be easier to remember them than to practice them, but through practice, you will see permanent change.

The basics build a foundation on which you can base all your living and decision making.

With the basics as a foundation for your life, you can go through challenges. The foundation will keep you during the challenge.

Let me be clear. I am talking about more than challenges with finances, relationships, and health. I'm talking about challenges with your thinking. When new teachings come your way, you can sort them based on your foundation. The three basic principles are your foundation.

Remember . . .

God loves you.
God wants your love.
God wants you to love others.

Now go out and do it.

ABOUT THE AUTHOR

Andrea Gadson is an author, blogger, workshop facilitator, and entrepreneur. She delivered insight, growth, and courage for Christian living. Her company, The SurrenderedPen, publishes life changing books in fiction and non-fiction arenas. She and her husband, Derik, reside in Southern New Jersey.

For more information visit
www.surrenderedpen.com

www.ingramcontent.com/pod-product-compliance
Lightning Source LLC
Chambersburg PA
CBHW041758040426
42447CB00001B/7